A History of Low Pleasant Quernmore

Mike Derbyshire

August 2017

Published August 2017

© Mike Derbyshire, 2017

Published by Rowton Books
Rowton Brook Farm
Quernmore, Lancaster LA2 9EQ

ISBN 978-0-9931689-4-9

Cover

View from the north-west: Rigg Farm is in the middle distance towards the right with Rock Cottages further to the right; Low Pleasant is higher up and further back towards the left.

Date stone of Joseph Kelsall at Low Pleasant farmhouse.

Detail from the first edition of the Ordnance Survey, dated 1844.

CONTENTS

Preface

List of Illustrations

Arrival of Kelsalls in Quernmore   1

Purchase of Rowton Brook   3

Enclosure of Quernmore Common   5

Creation of Low Pleasant   7

Farming New Rowton Brook   8

Involvement in Politics   12

Low Pleasant worked as a separate farm   14

Incorporation of tenancy of Dog and Partridge Farm   15

Expansion of Low Pleasant   21

PREFACE

These notes have been written at the suggestion of John Kelsall of Low Pleasant, to co-inside with the two-hundredth anniversary of the creation of Low Pleasant. They have been drafted in a fairly informal style, without including references to the sources of information. An annotated version is available, with references.

In these notes, amounts of money are given in pounds, shillings and pence, followed by the modern equivalent. Similarly, lengths are given in feet and metres. However, for simplicity, areas of land are given only in acres; one (statute) acre equals two fifths of a hectare. In general, family trees include people who survived childhood.

ILLUSTRATIONS

Figure 1	Family of Joseph and Margaret Kelsall	1
Figure 2	Family of Thomas and Dorothy Kelsall	3
Figure 3	Family of William and Mary Kelsall I	8
Figure 4	Family of Thomas and Betty Kelsall	11
Figure 5	Kelsalls who participated in the borough election of 1865	13
Figure 6	Family of William and Eleanor Kelsall	14
Figure 7	Family of Thomas and Mary Kelsall	17
Figure 8	Family of William and Mary Kelsall II	19
Figure 9	Family of Thomas and Alice Kelsall	21
Map 1	Rowton Brook in 1803	3
Map 2	Lots obtained by members of the Kelsall family	6
Map 3	Core land of Low Pleasant, 1817–24	7
Map 4	New Rowton Brook in 1824	9
Map 5	Dog and Partridge Farm in 1879	15
Map 6	Low Pleasant in 1909	17
Map 7	Core land of Low Pleasant in 1909	18
Map 8	Low Pleasant in 2017	23
Plate	Family of William Kelsall, late 1960s	24

ARRIVAL OF KELSALLS IN QUERNMORE

We know when the first Kelsall came to Quernmore: it was in 1687, during the short and troubled reign of King James II – a year before he was deposed in favour of William of Orange and Mary, in the 'Glorious Revolution'.

Janet Townson, the Quaker heroine of the story, had married Thomas Cragg of Wyresdale. After Thomas died, she married John Thompson and settled at Rowton Brook in Quernmore. (It is uncertain which of the two farms called Rowton Brook she and her second husband worked. The differentiation by spelling, as Rooten Brook and Rowton Brook, is comparatively recent.)

Janet's daughter, Elizabeth Cragg, married John Kelsall from Cheshire, who had settled in London. However, both John and Elizabeth died a few years later, leaving their two tiny sons, John and Joseph, as orphans. The boys' indomitable grandmother, Janet, rode to London and brought the two boys, aged two and three years, back to Rowton Brook in the paniers of her pony.

The elder Kelsall brother, John, moved away, but the younger brother, Joseph, settled in Quernmore and became the patriarch of the local Kelsalls. At the age of 41, he married Margaret Winder, then aged 25. Joseph and Margaret settled locally and in the 1740s they farmed what is now called Rooten Brook. The farm prospered, with 100 lambs on the slopes of Clougha Pike. Joseph took his turn serving in various offices, including acting as overseer for the poor for Quernmore.

Joseph and Margaret brought up a large family: three girls, Elizabeth, Ann and Margaret; and four boys, Joseph, William, John and Thomas (Figure 1). All their children married, with the wives of William and Thomas being sisters. Literacy was not universal at this time, even among reasonably prosperous farmers; for example, Thomas's wife, Dorothy, was unable to sign her name.

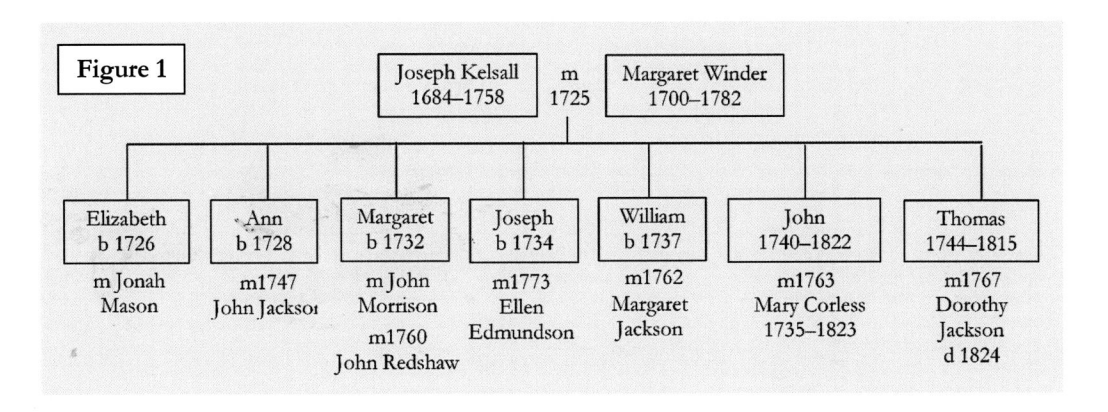

Figure 1

Joseph Kelsall (1684–1758) m 1725 Margaret Winder (1700–1782)

Children:
- Elizabeth b 1726 — m Jonah Mason
- Ann b 1728 — m1747 John Jackson
- Margaret b 1732 — m John Morrison; m1760 John Redshaw
- Joseph b 1734 — m1773 Ellen Edmundson
- William b 1737 — m1762 Margaret Jackson
- John 1740–1822 — m1763 Mary Corless 1735–1823
- Thomas 1744–1815 — m1767 Dorothy Jackson d 1824

The four boys all settled locally in Quernmore with their families: at various times, John and Mary farmed Rooten Brook; William and Margaret farmed Rowton Brook; and Thomas and Dorothy rented one of the farms in the nearby hamlet of Hare Appletree.

The Kelsall family were active Quakers. However, they were not always in good standing, for example as a result of getting married in the parish church at Lancaster. In contrast, their Quaker conviction was apparent when a ballot, held among the householders in Quernmore in 1757 to select a man to serve in the militia, fell on Joseph, the eldest son of Joseph and Margaret Kelsall; Joseph junior refused, as a Quaker, to serve. The matter was resolved by the householders of Quernmore setting up a subscription to pay for a substitute to stand in his place.

PURCHASE OF ROWTON BROOK

Thomas Kelsall (the youngest son of Joseph the patriarch and Margaret) and his wife Dorothy brought up three sons at Hare Appletree: William, Joseph and Thomas junior (Figure 2). The eldest son, William, married his first cousin, Mary Kelsall, the daughter of his uncle, John Kelsall. William and Mary were disowned by the Quakers for getting married in the parish church, but were later re-instated, together with their first two children. William's brother, Thomas junior, married Elizabeth Winder, also in the parish church. However, the third brother, Joseph, never married.

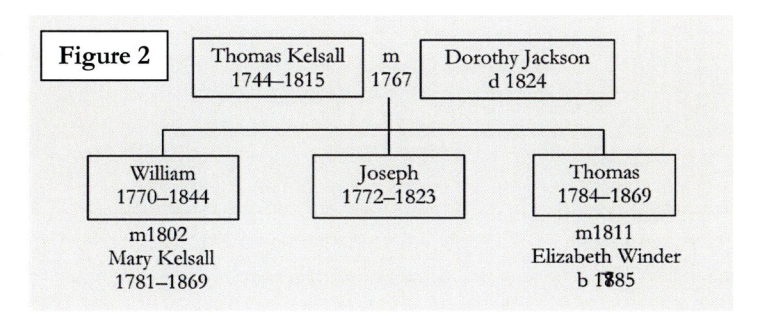

Figure 2

Thomas Kelsall 1744–1815 m 1767 Dorothy Jackson d 1824

- William 1770–1844 — m1802 Mary Kelsall 1781–1869
- Joseph 1772–1823
- Thomas 1784–1869 — m1811 Elizabeth Winder b 1785

At the turn of the nineteenth century, the Napoleonic Wars were causing a boom in agriculture. Thomas senior was certainly prospering and, in 1803, he bought Rowton Brook from George Fletcher for £1555. (It is difficult to provide a context for historical sums of money. However, a farm worker would then have been paid about 1s 7d, or 8p, per day.) Fletcher had bought the farm from the last of the Chapman family, who had owned it for well over a century. Thomas senior and Dorothy now moved from Hare Appletree to Rowton Brook as owner-occupiers, while Thomas junior and Elizabeth continued to farm at Hare Appletree.

A plan of Rowton Brook at this time is shown in Map 1. (Note that the background map was surveyed four decades later and includes many features that did not exist

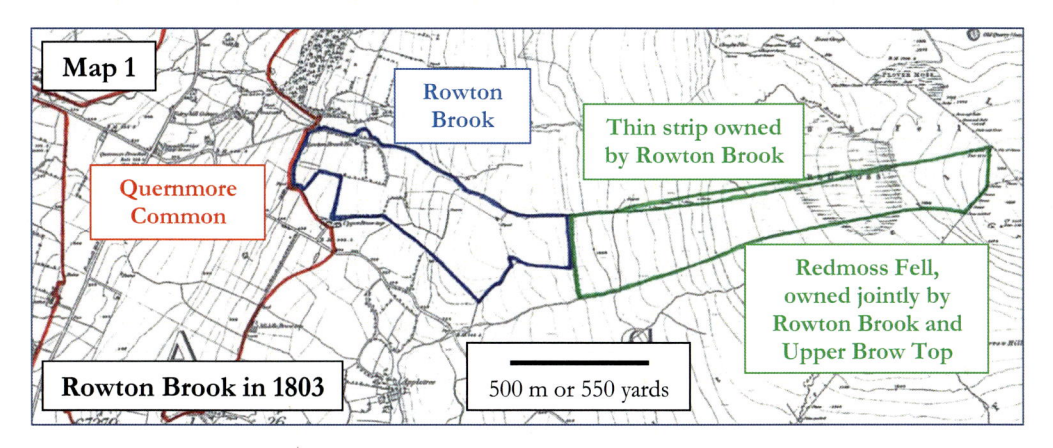

Map 1

Rowton Brook
Thin strip owned by Rowton Brook
Quernmore Common
Redmoss Fell, owned jointly by Rowton Brook and Upper Brow Top
Rowton Brook in 1803
500 m or 550 yards

in 1803.) The enclosed land at Rowton Brook (outlined in blue) lay between the unenclosed Quernmore Common to the west and Redmoss Fell to the east. To the north of Rowton Brook lay Rooten Brook farm, and beyond it Fell End. These were both similarly situated between Quernmore Common and the fell land. To the south lay Upper Brow Top and, beyond it, several farms at Hare Appletree, all again lying between the common and the fell.

At Rowton Brook, the enclosed land comprised 90 acres. Redmoss Fell was shared between Rowton Brook and Upper Brow Top, with Rowton Brook's share representing perhaps 70 acres. There was a very thin strip along the northern boundary of the joint fell which, rather curiously, belonged solely to Rowton Brook.

Redmoss Fell appears to have been unfenced at this date; it certainly was when the Ordnance Survey undertook its first survey of this area in 1844. It will therefore have been necessary for the boundary of the fell to have been carefully marked with boundary stones. Indeed some such stones have survived along the line of the boundary. Several of these are marked with '+ D'. Two stones on the north boundary have the letter 'J' inscribed on the north face. This will represent the Jepson family, who owned Rooten Brook, probably from 1631 until its ownership passed out of the family in 1816. One of these two stones has a 'K' inscribed on the south side, but this may have been added some time after the stones were first erected.

Thomas Kelsall senior died twelve years after buying Rowton Brook, leaving personal property (ie excluding land) to the value of £530 net. (For comparison, a farm worker would now be earning about 2s 2d, or 11p, per day.) The valuation of Thomas's property included £42 for horses and £340 for farming stock and implements. (The price of stock was very variable, but a cow might have then cost about £24 and a sheep about £1 – for animals which would have been considerably less productive than their modern counterparts.) Thomas bequeathed Rowton Brook jointly to his first and second sons, William and Joseph, while his third son, Thomas junior, inherited Bogman House and Moor Head, which lie just outside Quernmore in Over Wyresdale. It was the unmarried second son, Joseph, who was in occupation at Rowton Brook at this time, while William and Mary were farming at Moor Head and Thomas junior and Elizabeth were still farming at Hare Appletree.

ENCLOSURE OF QUERNMORE COMMON

One of the consequences of the agricultural boom that occurred during the Napoleonic Wars was an enthusiasm for the enclosure of common grazing land, so that it could be farmed more intensively and more profitably. Preparations for the enclosure of Quernmore Common were under way at the beginning of the nineteenth century and formal notices, announcing an intention to apply for an Act of Parliament to effect the enclosure, appeared in the *Lancaster Gazette* regularly from 1804 onwards. Progress was considerably slower in Quernmore than in neighbouring Scotforth, where the legal situation was much simpler. In Quernmore, interested parties included: the Duchy of Lancaster as the lord of the manor of Quernmore; the owners of land in Quernmore bordering the common with grazing and other rights on the common; the owners of land in the former 'vaccaries' in Quernmore, who claimed that their grazing land was not part of the common; the lord of the manor of Caton, who disputed the boundary between Quernmore and Caton to the north of Clougha Pike; the borough of Lancaster, who claimed ownership of part of the common; and various landowners in Lancaster and several villages lying north of the River Lune, who claimed extensive grazing rights on Quernmore Common.

Eventually agreement was reached between the various parties and the enclosure act was passed in 1811. Commissioners then started their laborious and complex work, including surveying the common, assessing the various claims to rights on the common, and allocating allotments to the successful claimants. They finally delivered their award at the King's Arms in Lancaster on 15 August 1817, by which time the agricultural boom was almost over.

Most of the allotments of enclosed land were allocated to landowners who had a claim to graze stock on the common. Thomas Kelsall senior received, as a consequence of his ownership of Rowton Brook, a block of 42 acres, comprising lots 9, 10 and 11 (Map 2 – again, the background map was surveyed much later).

Some lots were available for purchase, either from the commissioners (to pay for the cost of the enclosure process) or from landowners who wished to sell their allotments in advance of the award. The Kelsalls were energetic purchasers. Joseph (the second son of Thomas senior and Dorothy Kelsall – Figure 2) bought lot 7 (13 acres on Rigg Lane) and lot 13 (14½ acres on Quernmore Brow) from Richard Clark for £359 6d (£359.025). He also bought lot 12 (3 acres on Quernmore Brow) from Thomas Gibson for £52 9s (£52.45). Joseph's younger brother, Thomas junior (Figure 2), purchased lot 73 (8 acres on Little Fell Lane) from Richard Daker for £400. One other member of the Kelsall family was also involved in buying allotments. Joshua Kelsall, who was the son of Joseph, the eldest son of Joseph the patriarch and Margaret, purchased two tiny lots, 37 and 38 (¼ acre together), on the south side of Wyresdale Road to the west of Quernmore

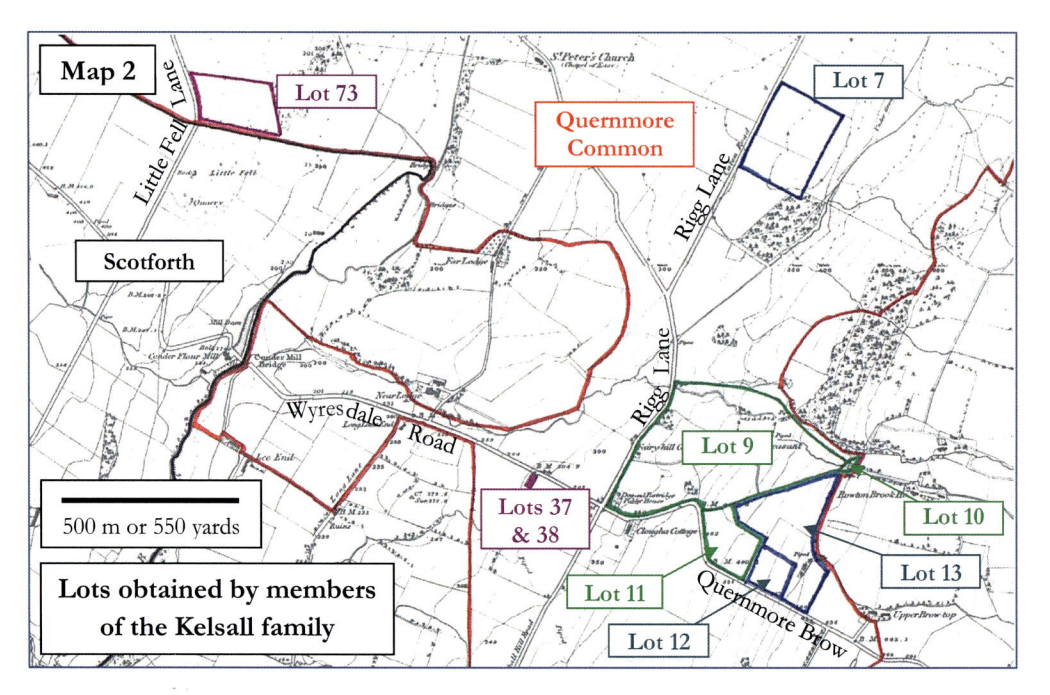

Crossroads. He bought these from John Carter and Thomas Brewer for £14 and £6 7s (£6.35) respectively.

The sums of money paid for these lots were considerable, especially in view of the additional expenditure required to make the land suitable for farming. For example, the £410, which Joseph Kelsall paid for a total of just over 30 acres, would have represented well over ten years' wages for a farm worker, and would have been sufficient to provide farm stock of say a dozen cows and 100 sheep. Joseph's brother, Thomas junior, paid a similar sum for a lot which was only about one quarter the size of Joseph's lots.

CREATION OF LOW PLEASANT

Thomas Kelsall senior did not live to see the enclosure take place; he had died two years earlier. As a result, the lots allocated to him passed, with Rowton Brook, to his two eldest sons, William and Joseph (Figure 2). Joseph was then in occupation at Rowton Brook and he set about building a new farm on the land that he and his father had acquired at the enclosure: lots 7, 9, 10, 11, 12 and 13 (a total of 73 acres). He undertook an enormous amount of work: building stone walls; diverting into culverts two becks which flowed across the land; and erecting the present farmhouse, complete with his date stone. Map 3 shows the core of the new farm, which became known as Low Pleasant. (Again, the background map was surveyed later.) It appears that Joseph's elder brother, William, and William's wife, Mary, returned briefly to work Rowton Brook as a separate farm.

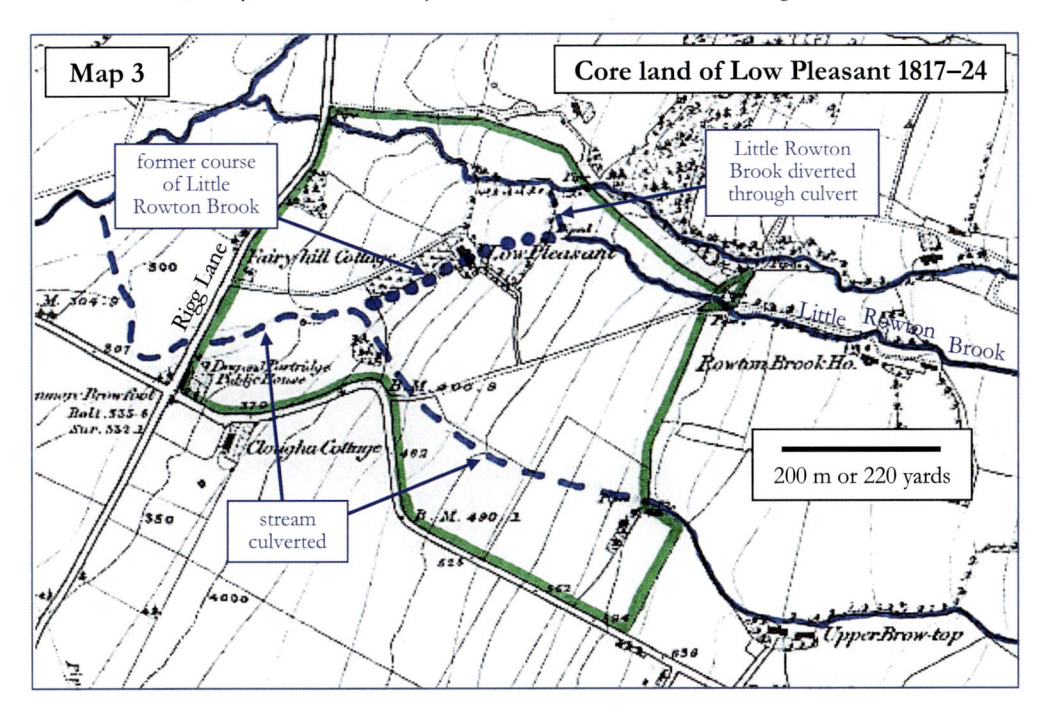

Map 3 — Core land of Low Pleasant 1817–24

Unfortunately, Joseph was not able to enjoy for long his hard-won new home; he died unmarried and intestate six years after the enclosure award, leaving £490 net. His property did not include any stock or farming implements, indicating that he was no longer working the farm himself when he died. His elder brother, William, inherited and became the sole owner of Low Pleasant and Rowton Brook. William and his wife, Mary, set about working the two farms together from Low Pleasant. The combined farm was known as New Rowton Brook and the original Rowton Brook became known as Old Rowton Brook.

FARMING NEW ROWTON BROOK

William and Mary Kelsall were now owner-occupiers of New Rowton Brook – Low Pleasant and Old Rowton Brook worked together as a single farm. They lived at Low Pleasant and brought up a large family there: five sons, Thomas, John, Joseph, William junior and Joshua; and two daughters, Margaret and Mary (Figure 3). The farmhouse at Old Rowton Brook was rented out.

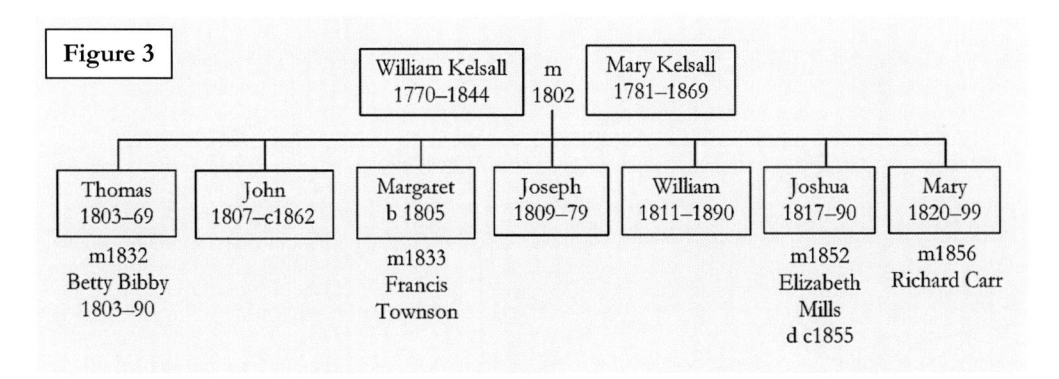

Figure 3

William Kelsall 1770–1844 m 1802 Mary Kelsall 1781–1869

- Thomas 1803–69 — m1832 Betty Bibby 1803–90
- John 1807–c1862
- Margaret b 1805 — m1833 Francis Townson
- Joseph 1809–79
- William 1811–1890
- Joshua 1817–90 — m1852 Elizabeth Mills d c1855
- Mary 1820–99 — m1856 Richard Carr

The eldest son, Thomas, married Betty Bibby. They farmed first at Hare Appletree in Quernmore and later at West View in Scotforth. Sons John, Joseph, and William junior never married. The youngest son, Joshua, married Elizabeth Mills, but she died within two or three years and they had no children. The elder daughter, Margaret, married Francis Townson and they settled locally. Mary, the younger daughter, married Richard Carr and they would later settle at Fell End in Quernmore.

A detailed map of Quernmore was prepared about 1824, in connection with a national initiative for the purpose of converting tithes from payment in kind to cash payments. The tithe map records that William senior and Mary's farm still comprised Low Pleasant combined with Old Rowton Brook (Map 4). It gives the extent of the farm as 234 acres (presumably about 90 acres at Old Rowton Brook, 70 acres at Low Pleasant and 70 acres from Redmoss Fell, owned jointly with Upper Brow Top).

The tithe map also shows that the land acquired by other members of the Kelsall family at the enclosure was still in their ownership. Thomas Kelsall (the youngest son of Thomas and Dorothy – Figure 2) was farming the former lot 73 himself and Joshua Kelsall (son of Joseph, the eldest son of Joseph the patriarch and Margaret) was renting out the former lots 37 and 38.

The north-western boundary of the land belonging to Low Pleasant still ran smoothly along Rigg Lane at this time (Map 3), with no buildings on the roadside. However, that was soon to change and, in 1826, William senior and Mary Kelsall built the Dog and Partridge Inn at the crossroads, adding their date stone. The first of two cottages next to the pub, later known as Rose Cottages, and a cottage at Fairy Hill

New Rowton Brook in 1824 — Map 4

New Rowton Brook

500 m or 550 yards

Thin strip owned by New Rowton Brook

Redmoss Fell, owned jointly with Upper Brow Top

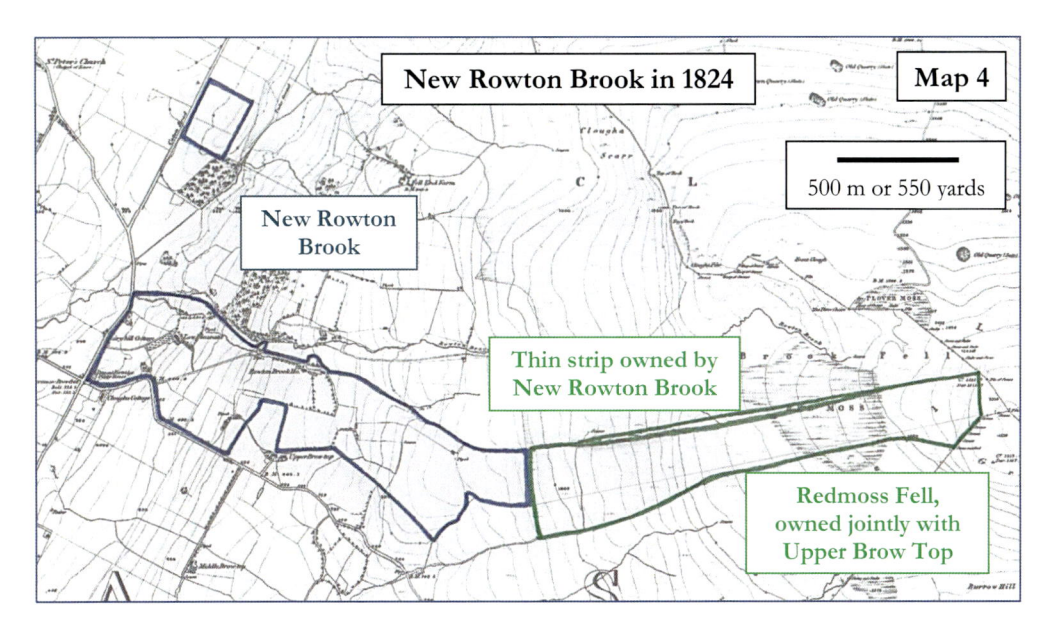

(further north along Rigg Lane) seem to have been built about the same time; they were certainly in existence by the time of the first national census in 1841. The nibbling away at the edge of Low Pleasant land on Rigg Lane continued, with Richard Carr, who had married Mary, the younger daughter of William senior and Mary Kelsall, building Rock Cottages in the early 1850s.

At the time of the first national census, William senior and Mary were living at Low Pleasant (aged about 70 and 60) together with three of their five sons, John, William junior and Joshua, and daughter Mary. There were also two servants living in. Subsequent censuses often show one servant living in at Low Pleasant. (The number of servants living out was not recorded.) Francis and Margaret Townson and their family were living at the Dog and Partridge Inn.

Two of the sons of William senior and Mary Kelsall were not present at Low Pleasant on the night of the census. Their eldest son, Thomas, was living at West View with his family. Regarding the remaining son, Joseph, we know that he was still living in Quernmore (probably based at Low Pleasant) from the records arising from his refusal to pay the church-rate, a local tax on all households to support the parish church. As a result, he was summoned to appear before the magistrates, who did not accept his justification that his refusal was based on his Quaker principles.

It was about this time that William Kelsall senior handed over management of the farm to the second and fourth of his five sons, John and William junior. He died in 1844, leaving personal property worth less than £100. (For comparison, the daily wage for a farm worker, which had fallen back a little, was now about 2s 1d or 10p.) In his will, William senior divided the farm in two, separating Low Pleasant from Old Rowton Brook. He bequeathed Low Pleasant and the Rigg allotment (the former lot 7) to his eldest and youngest sons, Thomas and Joshua; and bequeathed Old Rowton Brook, which now became known simply as Rowton Brook, to his other three sons, John, Joseph and William junior. The fell with its sheep was to be shared by the two farms. He left the Dog and Partridge Inn for the benefit of his daughter Margaret Townson (carefully excluding her husband) and her children. Rose Cottage, next to the Dog and Partridge, went to William senior's daughter Mary Carr.

William's will stipulated that the Low Pleasant and Rowton Brook estates were responsible for making substantial payments to his wife and younger daughter. Low Pleasant was particularly encumbered and was liable for paying £10 annually for life to William's daughter Mary and for paying £250 to be distributed between her children. Low Pleasant also shared with Rowton Brook liability for annual payments of £24 to William's wife, Mary, for the duration of her life.

The reference, in William Kelsall's will, to ownership of the fell suggests that Redmoss Fell, which had originally been jointly owned with Upper Brow Top, had, by this date, been divided physically between Rowton Brook and Upper Brow Top. Certainly, later maps show the former fell divided longitudinally into two unequal parts. (Compare Map 6 with Map 4.) The larger, more northerly part was called Rowton Brook Fell (or sometimes still Redmoss Fell) and was now owned jointly by Rowton Brook and Low Pleasant. This fell would later be fenced along both the north and south sides. A narrower piece of fell to the south, which comprised the rest of the fell formerly owned jointly by Rowton Brook and Upper Brow Top, was now owned by Upper Brow Top. This was not fenced from Hare Appletree Fell, which lay further to the south.

The three brothers who had inherited Rowton Brook, John, Joseph and William junior, promptly erected their date stone on the barn there. This is an unusual date stone, in that it appears to have been being inserted into the gable end after the construction of the wall, rather than incorporated over a doorway during the building of the barn, as was usual. Probably the brothers only modified the barn internally. It appears likely that a barn of this size would have been built during earlier, more prosperous times – probably following Thomas Kelsall's purchase of the farm in 1803, during the boom time for agriculture arising from the Napoleonic Wars. In scale, it is similar to the barn built at Low Pleasant by Joseph Kelsall when he developed Low Pleasant just over a decade later.

The first survey of this area undertaken by the Ordnance Survey was carried out in 1844. The resulting maps, which were at a scale of six inches to one mile, have been used as background for several of the maps in these notes. The line of the boundary of Quernmore, as determined by the Ordnance Survey at the eastern end of Redmoss Fell, was slightly different from that contained in the survey of 1824, with the result that Quernmore, and specifically Redmoss Fell, gained a little triangle of land.

At the time of the 1851 national census, Mary Kelsall (widow of William senior) was living at Low Pleasant and described herself as a land proprietor of 233 acres, which will refer to the total area of Low Pleasant, Rowton Brook and the fell. Living with her on census night were four of her five sons (all except Thomas, who had settled at West View), her daughter Mary and one of Margaret Townson's sons, William. The land at Rowton Brook continued to be farmed with Low Pleasant, principally by William junior. The farmhouse at Rowton Brook continued to be rented out. Francis and Margaret Townson remained as publicans at the Dog and Partridge.

Throughout this period, the eldest of the five brothers, Thomas, and his wife Betty farmed West View in Scotforth as a very prosperous farm, with five servants living in – three men and two women. They brought up a large family there: five sons, William, Edward, Thomas, Joseph and James; and one daughter, Mary – all of whom married (Figure 4).

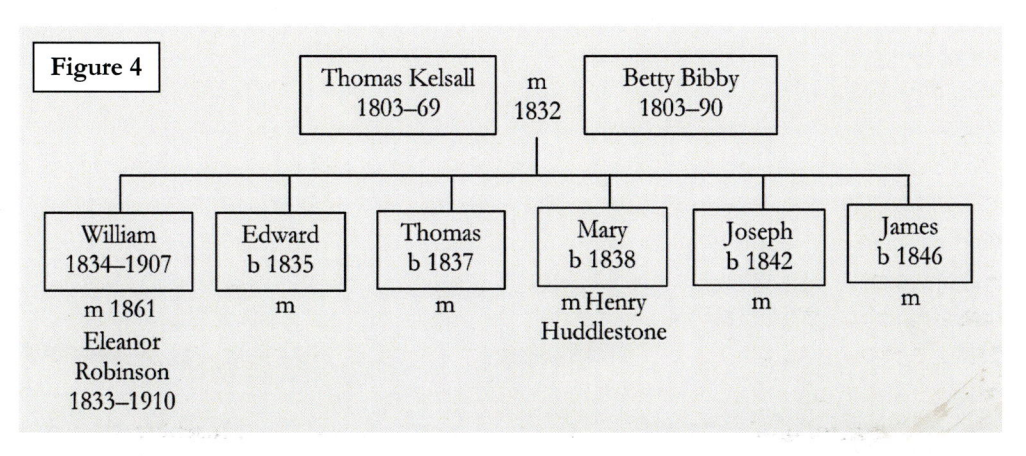

Figure 4

Thomas Kelsall 1803–69 m 1832 Betty Bibby 1803–90

- William 1834–1907 m 1861 Eleanor Robinson 1833–1910
- Edward b 1835 m
- Thomas b 1837 m
- Mary b 1838 m Henry Huddlestone
- Joseph b 1842 m
- James b 1846 m

When the eldest son of Thomas and Betty Kelsall, William (junior), married Eleanor Robinson in 1861, William and Eleanor settled at Low Pleasant and William's three uncles, John, Joseph and William (now senior) Kelsall (Figure 3), moved into their own property at Rowton Brook. The national census of that year shows William junior at Low Pleasant describing himself as farmer of 42 customary acres (equal to 68 statute acres) while uncle John, the oldest of the three brothers at Rowton Brook, described himself as farmer of 60 acres (equal to 97 statute acres). Old Mary Kelsall and her son Joshua had moved in with Richard and Mary Carr and their family at Fell End. Margaret Townson had apparently died and her widower, Francis, had moved out of the Dog and Partridge Inn with their family to settle at Narr Lodge, to the west of Low Pleasant, close to their Townson relatives.

INVOLVEMENT IN POLITICS

During the first half of the nineteenth century, many of the Kelsall men became freemen of the borough of Lancaster; generally as soon as they reached the age of 21, the age of majority. This 'freedom' could be obtained in one of three ways: by being the son of a freeman; by being apprenticed to a freeman; or by purchase – presumably the early Kelsalls obtained their freedom by the last of these methods. The status of freeman provided some practical advantages. You did not have to pay the tolls paid by outsiders in connection with Lancaster market and, perhaps most importantly, you could vote in the famously corrupt elections that the borough held for its two parliamentary seats.

All three sons of Thomas and Dorothy Kelsall (William, Joseph and Thomas – Figure 2) became freemen of Lancaster. Voting was a very public affair; indeed, there was little point in a politician bribing voters in the borough elections unless he could be sure how they actually voted. Poll books were published after each election, listing all the voters and the candidates that they had voted for. In the election of 1818, when three candidates, two Conservative and one Liberal, stood for the two seats, all three of the Kelsall brothers voted for only one candidate, the Conservative John Fenton Cawthorne. He had been successful in previous Lancaster elections, but was unsuccessful in 1818. Cawthorne was one of the most disreputable candidates (in a very strong field) ever to stand for election at Lancaster.

Moving on a generation, all five sons of William and Mary Kelsall (Thomas, John, Joseph, William and Joshua – Figure 3) became freemen. Generally, the five brothers did not all vote the same way. However, there were exceptions: in 1848 and 1864, when they all voted Liberal; and in 1857, when they all split their support, voting for a Liberal and for a Conservative.

(Because of their ownership or tenancy of landed property, several of these Kelsalls were able to vote in the county elections, as well as in the borough elections. William and Thomas Kelsall, two of the sons of Thomas and Dorothy (Figure 2), were qualified as owners of Low Pleasant and the former lot 73 respectively. In addition, Thomas Kelsall, the eldest son of William and Mary (Figure 3), was qualified by being the occupier of a large farm at Hare Appletree. Later, John, Joseph, William and Joshua, the four younger sons of William and Mary (Figure 3), were likewise able to vote in the county elections, based on their part ownership of Low Pleasant or Rowton Brook.)

Returning to consider the freemen of Lancaster and moving on another generation, William, Edward, Thomas, Joseph and James Kelsall, the five sons of Thomas and Betty at West View (Figure 4), all became freemen as they came of age, and voted in the borough elections. Their voting pattern was fairly clear: they all voted the same way, generally for the Liberals, but sometimes they all split their vote, supporting a Liberal and a Conservative candidate.

In the notorious Lancaster election of 1865, there were three candidates for the two seats: E M Fenwick and H W Schneider for the Liberals; and E Lawrence for the Conservatives. Several of the Kelsalls from Low Pleasant and Rowton Brook voted in this election (Figure 5). Four were sons of William (who had died two decades earlier) and Mary Kelsall: Thomas (senior) at West View, Joseph (senior) of Rowton Brook, William (senior) of Rowton Brook and Joshua. (John, the second son of William and Mary, appears to have died by now; it is likely that he was the Kelsall who hanged himself at the low barn at Fell End.) The younger generation was represented by three of the sons of Thomas senior and Betty Kelsall: William (junior) at Low Pleasant, Thomas (junior) at West View and Joseph (junior), who had just moved from West View to Hala Carr in Scotforth. Everyone, except William senior, voted for the two Liberals. William senior split his vote, supporting the Liberal Fenwick and the Conservative Lawrence.

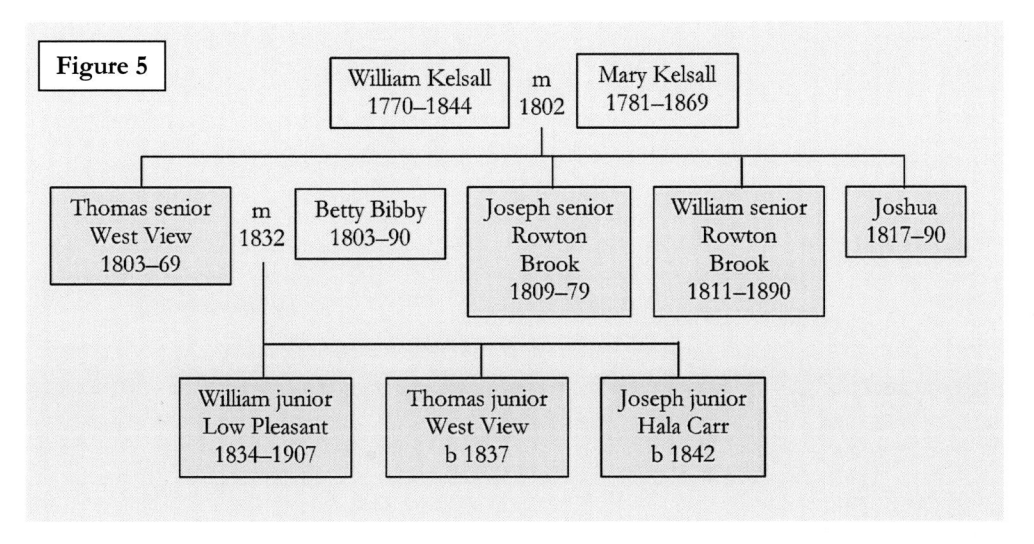

Figure 5

```
                William Kelsall  m    Mary Kelsall
                1770–1844       1802  1781–1869
```

Thomas senior, West View, 1803–69 — m 1832 — Betty Bibby, 1803–90
Joseph senior, Rowton Brook, 1809–79
William senior, Rowton Brook, 1811–1890
Joshua, 1817–90

Children of Thomas senior and Betty Bibby:
William junior, Low Pleasant, 1834–1907
Thomas junior, West View, b 1837
Joseph junior, Hala Carr, b 1842

The level of corruption at this election was so spectacular that a commission was set up to investigate the allegations of bribery. As practicing Quakers, the Kelsalls all gave evidence by affirmation, rather than on oath. Except for the two Thomases, they all admitted that they had been paid for their vote. William senior of Rowton Brook had received £5 from the Conservatives. The other four had each received money from the Liberals: Joseph senior of Rowton Brook, £3; Joshua, £2 5s (£2.25); William junior of Low Pleasant, £10; and Joseph junior of Hala Carr, £3 10s (£3.50). These sums were by no means exceptional, although William junior's £10 was towards the upper end of the range of amounts that voters generally received. (For comparison, at that date, an agricultural worker would have had to work for about three months to earn £10, which would now have been enough to buy perhaps five sheep.) The commissioners found that there had been extensive bribery and, as a consequence, Lancaster was disenfranchised and lost its parliamentary representation for nearly twenty years.

LOW PLEASANT WORKED AS A SEPARATE FARM

Low Pleasant was now being worked by William and Eleanor Kelsall as a farm in its own right, independent of Rowton Brook. The farm was owned jointly by William's father, Thomas Kelsall of West View, and his uncle Joshua Kelsall (Figures 3 and 4).

The Quakers were flourishing in Quernmore and a 'meeting', which will have met in people's houses, was established there in 1860. Three years later, Thomas and Joshua Kelsall gave one eighth of an acre of steeply-sloping land by Rigg Lane to the Quakers for a burial ground and for the building of a meeting house.

Thomas Kelsall of West View died in 1869, leaving a personal estate of £1340 net. (For comparison, a cow was now worth about £14 and a sheep £2.) He had retired from farming, since his property did not include any farm stock or implements. His half share of Low Pleasant went to his wife, Betty, for her life, and then to their son, William of Low Pleasant (Figure 4). The Low Pleasant estate was charged with bequests of £110 each to William's four brothers and sister, to be paid following the death of their mother, Betty. Thomas and, later, his wife Betty were buried in the Quaker burial ground.

William (now referred to as senior) and Eleanor brought up three sons at Low Pleasant, Thomas, James Robinson and William junior, all of whom married (Figure 6).

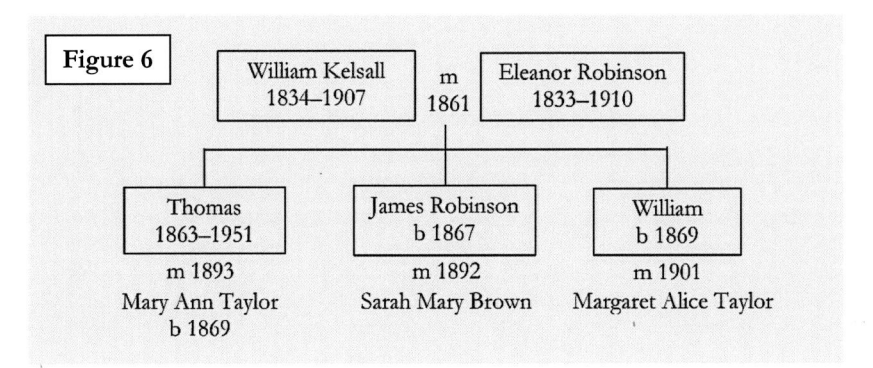

Figure 6

William Kelsall 1834–1907 m 1861 Eleanor Robinson 1833–1910

- Thomas 1863–1951 — m 1893 Mary Ann Taylor b 1869
- James Robinson b 1867 — m 1892 Sarah Mary Brown
- William b 1869 — m 1901 Margaret Alice Taylor

At the time of the 1871 national census, William senior and Eleanor Kelsall were occupying Low Pleasant, a farm of 69 acres, with their three young sons. William senior's uncle, Joseph Kelsall (the third of the five brothers – Figure 3), was now living in one of the Rock Cottages. Francis Townson, the widower of William senior's aunt Margaret, was now living at Kelbrick Farm in Barnacre near Garstang with their younger children. Thomas Townson, one of the older sons of Francis and Margaret, was the tenant at Rowton Brook, where he lived with his wife, Esther, and their family. The Carr family were still at Fell End, although old Mary Kelsall (William senior's grandmother) had died two years earlier. Joshua Kelsall (William senior's uncle, the youngest of the five brothers) had moved back to Low Pleasant. He was living there when he made his will in 1869, but was absent on census night, visiting his Townson relatives in Barnacre.

INCORPORATION OF TENANCY OF
DOG AND PARTRIDGE FARM

The land to the north-west of Low Pleasant, lying between it and Narr Lodge, was known as Dog and Partridge Farm (Map 5). This had been formed by combining six allotments made to three different landowners at the enclosure of Quernmore Common in 1817. It came to be owned by Christopher Johnson, surgeon, of Lancaster.

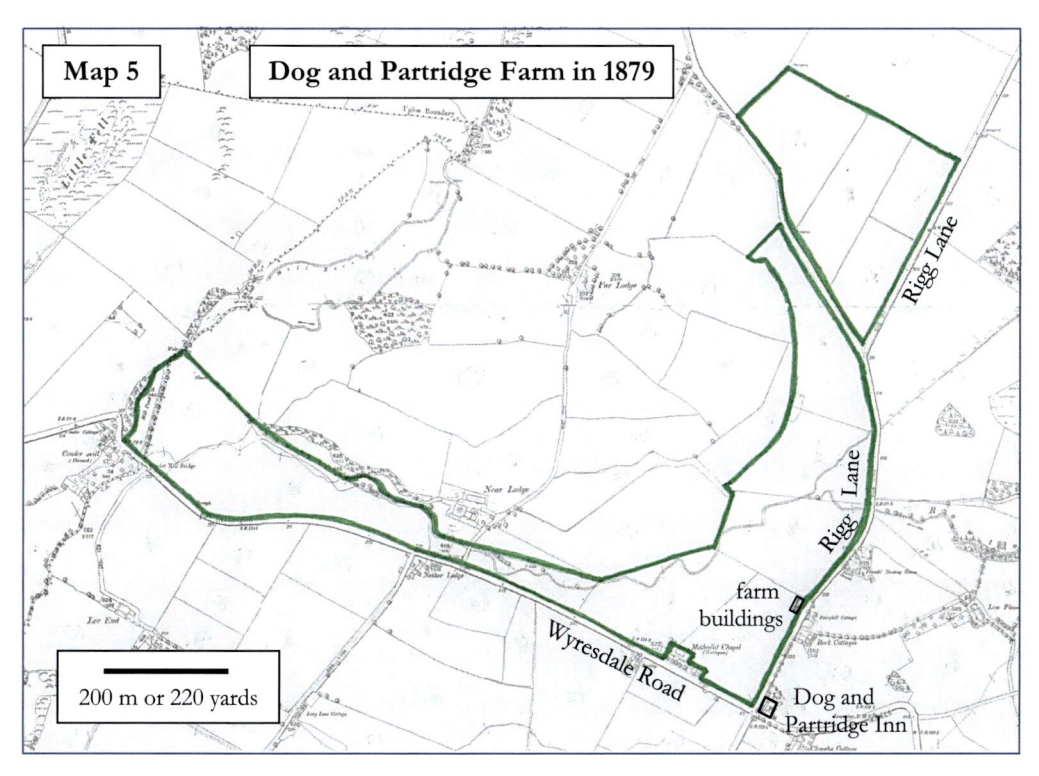

Map 5 — Dog and Partridge Farm in 1879

200 m or 220 yards

In 1879, William Kelsall senior of Low Pleasant (Figure 6) took over the tenancy and stock of Dog and Partridge Farm from John Mason for £550 and agreed to pay Johnson a rent of £90 per annum. The tenancy included farm buildings on Rigg Lane, at the eastern edge of the farm, but no farmhouse. A plot of half an acre beside Wyresdale Road, on the southern edge of the farm, had by then been sold for a Methodist graveyard and chapel. No buildings at the Dog and Partridge Inn belonged to the farm.

At the time of the 1881 national census, William senior and Eleanor Kelsall and their family continued in occupation at Low Pleasant. William referred to himself as a farmer of 150 acres – presumably a combination of Low Pleasant and Dog and Partridge Farm. In the trade directories, he described himself as a yeoman. The census return records that William senior's uncle, William Kelsall (the fourth of the five brothers –

Figure 3), had moved in with his Townson tenants at Rowton Brook, where he described himself as a gentleman.

In December 1888, the contract was let for work on the section of the Thirlmere Aqueduct that would pass through Low Pleasant. The tunnel was excavated by 'cut and cover' with the aqueduct itself being made of concrete, seven feet (2.1 m) wide and seven feet high to a domed roof. The many workmen involved in digging this enormous trench and constructing the concrete tunnel were, according to the official view, well provided for and well behaved. However, the local view appears to have been that they caused considerable dislocation in the village, one consequence of which was the conversion of the Dog and Partridge Inn into the Temperance Hotel. Another legacy of the aqueduct is the short length of stone channel that was constructed so that Rowton Brook (the bigger of the two becks) can act as an emergency flow. These works are just above the point where a culvert brings Little Rowton Brook into the main Rowton Brook, diverting it from its earlier course through the site of the buildings of Low Pleasant (see Map 3).

In 1890, William senior's mother Betty (Figure 4) and his uncle Joshua (the youngest of the five brothers – Figure 3) both died, following which William inherited all of Low Pleasant. Joshua left personal property of only £174 net, which was insufficient to pay the specific bequests in his will. His brother, Joseph (of Rowton Brook), had left a similar amount when he had died ten years earlier. On the other hand, brother William (of Rowton Brook), who was the last of the five to die (also in 1890), left personal property worth £1030. In Joshua's will, the bequest of his half of Low Pleasant to his nephew William was charged with payments of £80 each to ten of Joshua's nephews and nieces, and with two other payments, one of £100 to Joshua's sister-in-law and one of £19 19s (£19.95) to a friend. (A cow might now be worth roughly £12 and a sheep possibly £2. A farm worker was now earning about 3s 4d, or 17p, per day.) The three brothers, Joshua, Joseph and William, were all buried in the Quaker burial ground in Quernmore.

The records of the 1891 national census show that William senior and Eleanor Kelsall were still living at Low Pleasant, with their three sons, who were then in their 20s. The Dog and Partridge Inn, or Temperance Hotel, now incorporated a post office.

Soon afterwards, William senior handed over the management of Low Pleasant to his eldest son, Thomas (Figure 6), and William and Eleanor moved to one of the Rock Cottages. In 1903, William Kelsall senior sold an acre of land to John McAdam, who built on it the Indian-style Bungalow, which was demolished in about 2010.

William senior died in 1907, leaving Low Pleasant and half the fell, with 50 sheep, to his eldest son, Thomas. Under William's will, Low Pleasant was charged with paying £130 per annum to his wife, Eleanor, during her life; and with paying £150 to their second son, James Robinson, and £300 to their third son, William junior. William senior and Eleanor were buried in the Quaker burial ground.

Figure 7

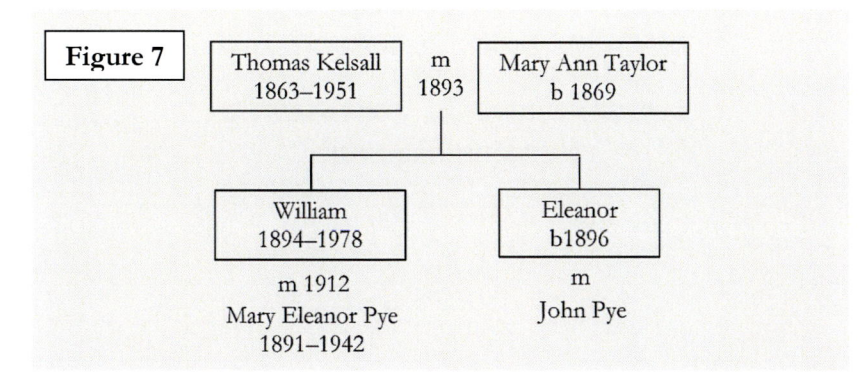

```
Thomas Kelsall    m      Mary Ann Taylor
  1863–1951      1893        b 1869
         |
    ┌────┴────┐
 William      Eleanor
 1894–1978    b1896
   m 1912       m
Mary Eleanor Pye  John Pye
  1891–1942
```

William Kelsall senior's eldest son, Thomas, had married Mary Ann Taylor in 1893 and they settled at Low Pleasant. There they brought up their family, comprising a son, William, and a daughter, Eleanor (Figure 7). The children both married; William's wife, Mary, and Eleanor's husband, John, were sister and brother.

A national survey undertaken in 1909 shows 72 acres of enclosed land at Low Pleasant, plus 39 acres representing half of the fell land (Maps 6 and 7). Thomas and Mary Kelsall were recorded as working Low Pleasant as owner-occupiers.

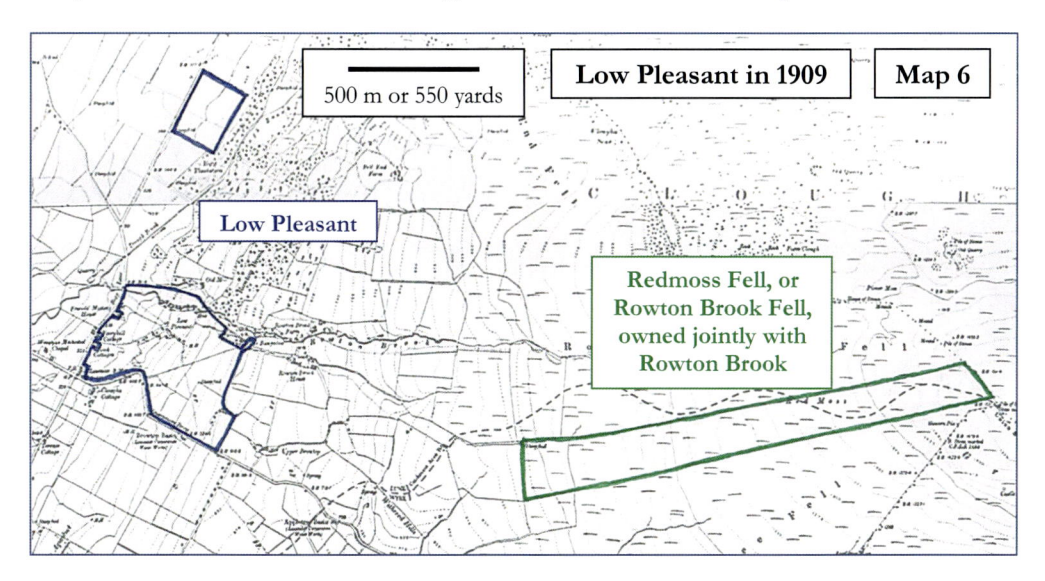

Map 6 — Low Pleasant in 1909

500 m or 550 yards

Labels: Low Pleasant; Redmoss Fell, or Rowton Brook Fell, owned jointly with Rowton Brook

Thomas Kelsall had taken over the tenancy of Dog and Partridge Farm, the ownership of which had passed to Alice Johnson, the niece of Christopher Johnson. Thomas paid a rent of £75 per annum – £15 less than his father had paid Christopher Johnson thirty years earlier.

Rowton Brook was now owned by Townsons and was tenanted. The highest field of the enclosed land of Rowton Brook, which was known as High Coppy and contained

Map 7 — Core land of Low Pleasant in 1909

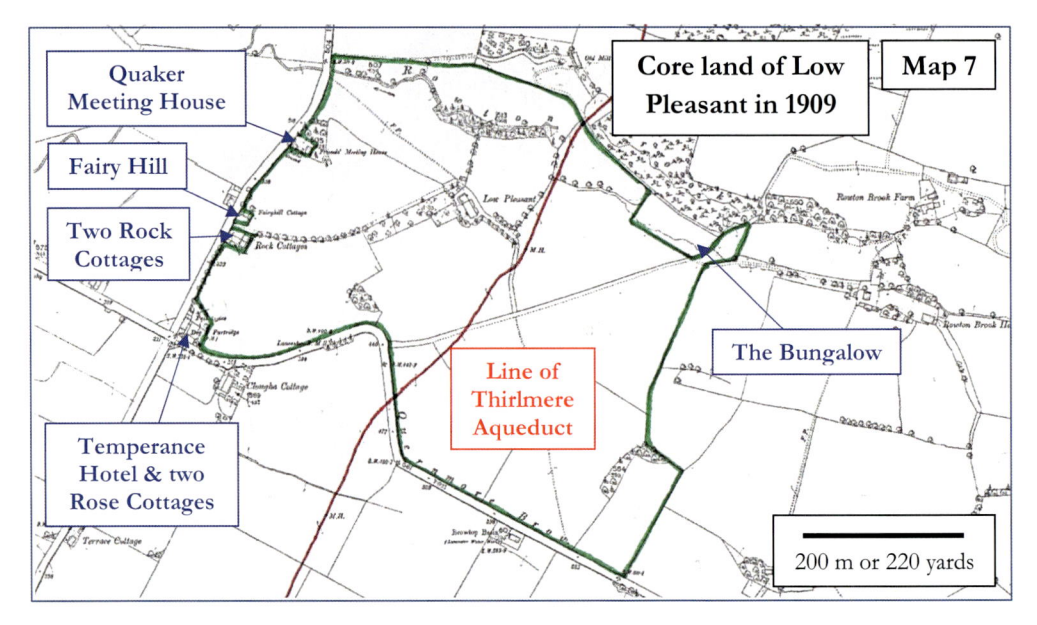

Labels: Quaker Meeting House; Fairy Hill; Two Rock Cottages; Temperance Hotel & two Rose Cottages; Line of Thirlmere Aqueduct; The Bungalow. Scale: 200 m or 220 yards.

14 acres, had reverted to fell land, although it was not incorporated into the joint fell shared between Rowton Brook and Low Pleasant.

The national census of 1911 (the last for which records are open to the public) found Thomas and Mary Kelsall and their two teenage children still at Low Pleasant. In a directory for 1913, Thomas described himself as a yeoman and added that he was overseer of the poor (for Quernmore).

In 1919, Thomas and Mary Kelsall left Low Pleasant and moved to one of the Rock Cottages. Their son, William, took over the farm with his wife, Mary.

In about 1920, Thomas Kelsall sold a small piece of land to the east of the Bungalow to Harry Titley Morris, who had succeeded McAdam as owner of the Bungalow. This deprived the field of the beck, Little Rowton Brook, so Morris provided a water trough and sheepfold by way of compensation. Thomas also sold a more substantial piece of land to Morris – the two fields of 13 acres that constituted lot 7 at the enclosure of Quernmore Common in 1817. Thomas considered that these two fields were useless for producing grass, because of the infestation of rabbits.

William (now senior) and Mary Kelsall raised a large family at Low Pleasant, but suffered considerable misfortune. Two children died in childhood, while six survived: three sons, Thomas, William junior and George; and three daughters, Eleanor, Mary and Dorothy (Figure 8). All the children married, but George died at the age of 23. This was the second time that a William and Mary Kelsall had brought up a family at Low Pleasant; the first was when William's great-great-grandfather and mother lived there a hundred years earlier (Figure 3).

Figure 8

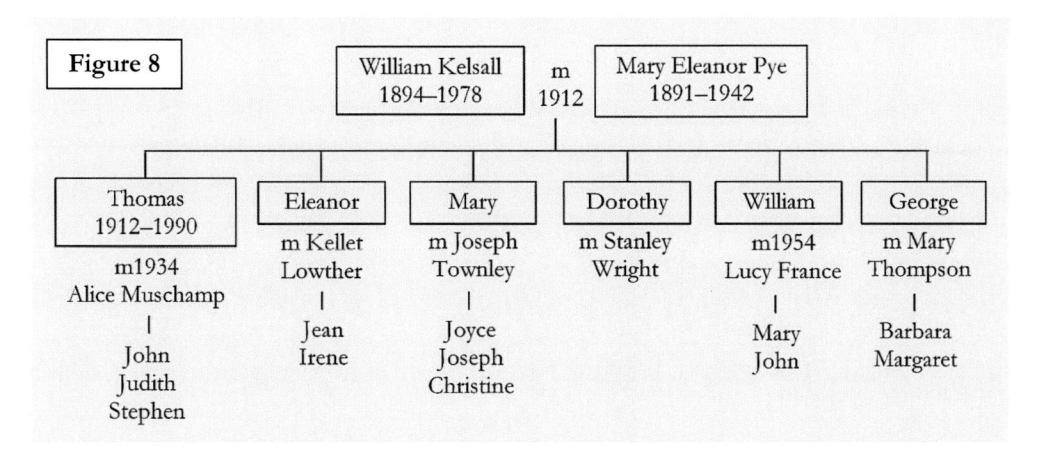

```
William Kelsall  m   Mary Eleanor Pye
  1894–1978    1912      1891–1942
```

Thomas 1912–1990	Eleanor	Mary	Dorothy	William	George
m1934 Alice Muschamp	m Kellet Lowther	m Joseph Townley	m Stanley Wright	m1954 Lucy France	m Mary Thompson
John Judith Stephen	Jean Irene	Joyce Joseph Christine		Mary John	Barbara Margaret

As the Second World War dragged on into 1941, the government became concerned about the need to produce more food. In this context, it undertook a survey of the state of farms and the standards of husbandry. The resulting reports are now open to the public. William Kelsall senior was recorded as the occupier of Low Pleasant, a farm of 58 acres with 35 acres of rough grazing. The farm was owned by his father, Thomas, living at Rock Cottage. Comments were provided on the facilities available at Low Pleasant, including the condition of the house, farm buildings, roads, ditches, drainage and fences. These were all described as good. The water supply still came from the stream, but the farm did have electricity. Perhaps the most important part of the survey was an assessment of the management of the farm; William was classified as 'A', as were most farmers. It was noted that William also tenanted Dog and Partridge Farm, containing 61 acres.

The report dealing with the situation at Rowton Brook was something of a contrast. The farm was now owned by Harry Morris and tenanted by Dick Barber. It was recorded as comprising 88 acres of enclosed land with 99 acres of rough grazing, which seems to have been something of an exaggeration. The state of the facilities was more mixed than at Low Pleasant. Although the buildings and ditches were good, the fences and drainage were only fair and the roads were poor. Again the water supply came from the stream, but there was no electricity installed. The management of the farm was classed as 'B', because of a combination of personal factors.

William Kelsall senior's wife, Mary, died in 1942, aged 50. Two years later, William married Elizabeth (Bessie) Winder. Bessie had been a servant girl at Low Pleasant in the 1920s. She later became a district nurse and midwife, until she married William.

Thomas, the eldest son of William senior and Mary, had married Alice Muschamp in 1934. He took over the tenancy of Dog and Partridge Farm, which was now called Rigg Farm, in 1943 and farmed the land from a cottage at Narr Lodge.

Alice Johnson, the owner of Rigg Farm, died the same year and the farm was put up for auction. Thomas Kelsall hoped to buy the farm, but was outbid at the auction by

Harry Morris. However, Thomas continued to lease the farm and Morris built a farmhouse for him near the farm buildings on Rigg Lane.

Morris had built up a considerable holding of farms in the locality. As well as Dog and Partridge Farm, or Rigg Farm, these included Fell End, Rooten Brook, Rowton Brook and Upper Brow Top. He also owned the Bungalow, the Temperance Hotel, both Rose Cottages and the Rock Cottage lying nearer to the Temperance Hotel. Indeed, Low Pleasant stood out in independent isolation, surrounded by Morris land.

The bulk of Morris's land passed to his son, Rupert, and, on his death, to Rupert's widow, Vera Cecilia Morris. An exception was the Lea, which comprised the two most westerly fields in Rigg Farm and contained 14 acres. Harry Morris had sold this to J Bibby and Sons in 1946.

EXPANSION OF LOW PLEASANT

In the mid-1940s, William Kelsall senior (Figure 8) purchased Lower Langthwaite farm in Scotforth and farmed it with Low Pleasant. He also bought much of the Lea, at the eastern end of Rigg Farm, from Bibbys. His father, Thomas Kelsall of Rock Cottage, died in 1951 and left Low Pleasant to him. Three years later, he built a bungalow at Lower Langthwaite, called Pleasant View, where he and his second wife, Bessie, went to live. At the same time, William senior's second son, William junior, married Lucy France and took over the farming of Low Pleasant.

A photograph of William Kelsall senior's grown-up family is shown in the plate on page 24.

Thomas, the eldest son of William Kelsall senior, and Thomas's wife, Alice, continued to work Rigg Farm, where they brought up their three children, John, Judith and Stephen (Figure 9).

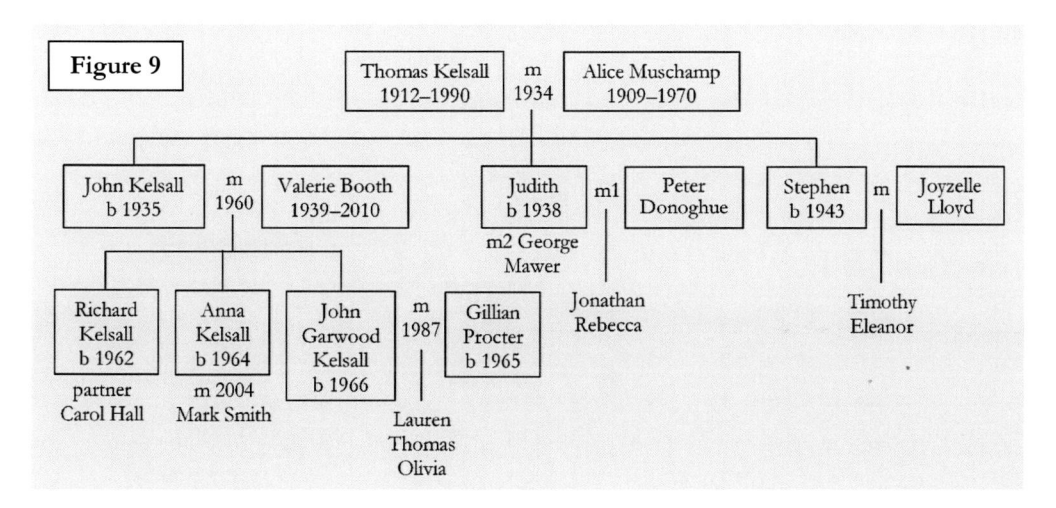

Figure 9

Thomas Kelsall 1912–1990 m 1934 Alice Muschamp 1909–1970

- John Kelsall b 1935 m 1960 Valerie Booth 1939–2010
  - Richard Kelsall b 1962 — partner Carol Hall
  - Anna Kelsall b 1964 — m 2004 Mark Smith
  - John Garwood Kelsall b 1966 — m 1987 Gillian Procter b 1965
    - Lauren
    - Thomas
    - Olivia
- Judith b 1938 m1 Peter Donoghue; m2 George Mawer
  - Jonathan
  - Rebecca
- Stephen b 1943 m Joyzelle Lloyd
  - Timothy
  - Eleanor

In the mid-1960s, the government instigated a register of common land under the Commons Registration Act. Walter Drinkwater, now the owner of Upper Brow Top, applied to have Redmoss Fell, or Rowton Brook Fell, designated as common land. The area involved comprised both the fell shown in Map 6 and High Coppy, the most easterly field of Rowton Brook: a total of 93 acres. Since this claim was not disputed, the registration of the fell as common land became final. Drinkwater further claimed that Upper Brow Top had the right to graze 140 sheep on the whole of this common land. Since this was again not disputed, the registration of this right became final. Bizarrely, Dick Barber, who was the tenant at Rowton Brook, registered his right to graze 70 sheep on Redmoss Fell – land that was part of his own tenancy.

The ownership of Redmoss Fell was registered to Vera Morris, the owner of Rowton Brook. Again, this was not disputed and became final. The strip of fell to the south of Redmoss Fell, owned by Upper Brow Top, was unfenced from Hare Appletree Fell and was considered to be part of that fell. Ownership of this strip was registered to Upper Brow Top.

In 1963, Thomas's brother, William junior, and his wife, Lucy (Figure 8), moved from Low Pleasant to Lower Langthwaite. At the same time, Thomas's son, John, and John's wife, Valerie, came to Low Pleasant, where they brought up their family of three children, Richard, Anna and Garwood (Figure 9).

William Kelsall senior died in 1977. His will provided for his wife during her lifetime and then left Low Pleasant and the Lea to his elder son, Thomas, and Lower Langthwaite to his younger son, William junior, with bequests of similar value to his other children.

Two years later, Thomas, who had been a widower since Alice died in 1970, converted an out-building at Low Pleasant into a cottage for his retirement.

In 1982, Vera Morris put Rowton Brook up for sale. John bought two fields, Rowton Meadow and Stoney Paddock. Six years later, John and Garwood bought Rigg Farm. The land involved had been somewhat truncated (from its earlier existence as Dog and Partridge Farm) by the sale of the land at the western end (known as the Lea and now owned by Thomas) and by the sale of land for housing along Wyresdale Road.

Thomas Kelsall died in 1990. He left Low Pleasant to his son John and the rest of his property, including the Lea, to his other two children, Judith and Stephen. A few years later, they sold the Lea. A plot of about two acres was bought by Quernmore Recreation Club, who have built on it a bowling green, tennis court and club house.

John Kelsall was eventually able to rationalise the position regarding Redmoss Fell, or Rowton Brook Fell. Low Pleasant had not made use of its half share in the fell for many years; indeed John's grandfather, William senior (Figure 8), had not even registered his part ownership of the fell under the Commons Registration Act during the 1960s. Despite this, John succeeded in establishing his right and, in 1992, sold his half share of the fell to the Duke of Westminster.

John and Valerie Kelsall moved out of Low Pleasant and into Rigg farmhouse in 1990 and their son, Garwood, and his wife, Gill, moved into the farmhouse at Low Pleasant. Nineteen years later, John and Valerie moved into the cottage at Low Pleasant.

At about the same time, Garwood Kelsall bought two fields from Narr Lodge, called Moss Meadow and Dobbies, to add to the land of Rigg Farm.

To bring the story up to date, John and Garwood together continue to work the land of the expanded Low Pleasant. John owns the land from the original Low Pleasant and the two fields from Rowton Brook, while Garwood now owns the land at Rigg Farm and the two fields from Narr Lodge. Garwoood's sister, Anna, owns the farmhouse at Rigg Farm. A plan of the land belonging to Low Pleasant in August 2017 is shown in Map 8.

Map 8 — **Low Pleasant in 2017**

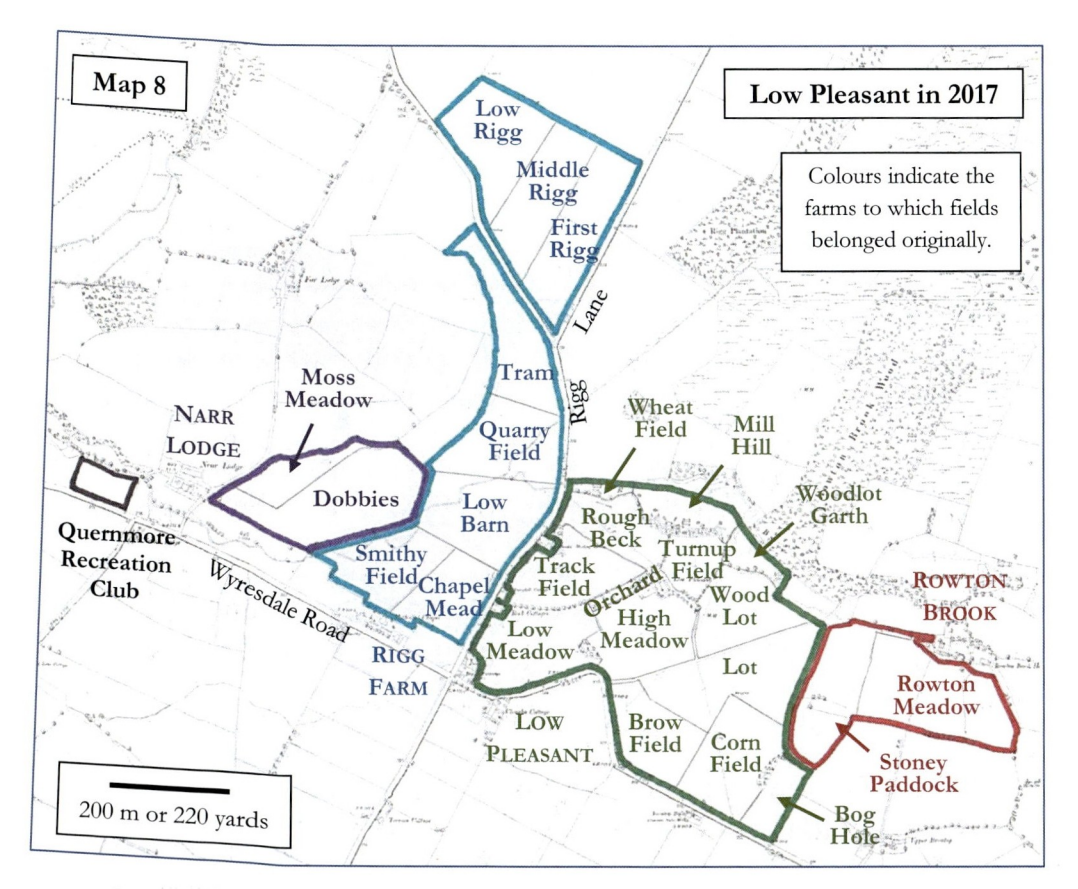

Colours indicate the farms to which fields belonged originally.

Field labels on map: Low Rigg, Middle Rigg, First Rigg, Moss Meadow, Tram, Quarry Field, Wheat Field, Mill Hill, Woodlot Garth, NARR LODGE, Dobbies, Low Barn, Rough Beck, Turnup Field, Quernmore Recreation Club, Smithy Field, Chapel Mead, Track Field, Orchard, Wood Lot, ROWTON BROOK, Wyresdale Road, Low Meadow, High Meadow, Rowton Meadow, RIGG FARM, LOW PLEASANT, Brow Field, Corn Field, Stoney Paddock, Bog Hole, Rigg Lane.

200 m or 220 yards

There is an interesting historical contrast within the fields that now make up Low Pleasant. The fields of Rigg Farm, like those of the original Low Pleasant, were enclosed two hundred years ago, following the Quernmore Enclosure Award of 1817. In contrast, the fields of Narr Lodge, like those of Rowton Brook, had been enclosed many centuries earlier. In the case of Narr Lodge, fields were first carved out in the late thirteenth century, from what was then the forest land of the first Earl of Lancaster. Fields were probably established even earlier at Rowton Brook.

Plate: Family of William Kelsall, late 1960s (see Figure 8 and pages 18–19)
From left to right: William Kelsall junior, Lucy Kelsall, Thomas Kelsall, Joseph Townley, Alice Kelsall, Mary Townley, William Kelsall senior, Mary Kelsall, Bessie Kelsall, Eleanor Lowther, Stanley Wright, Kellet Lowther, Dorothy Wright